The Interviews:

Tales from the Delaware Paranormal Community.

A collection of tales offered to

E. Byrd

with help from

The Oddporium, The Gallery of the Peculiar and the Bizarre.

Wilmington, DE

ISBN-13:

978-1541271708

ISBN-10:

154127170X

Index

Forward

Many years ago, I was the host of many haunted locations in a small town in Ohio. I had been seen on many national paranormal TV shows and was making a steady living from the field. I am now retired from the paranormal field with the exception of the odd par-con speaking engagement tossed in here and there. This book originally was offered to someone else, and I would ghostwrite the content, offering all credits as legally possible. After a period of paranoia on the part of the family, this book was then left to myself to finish. I decided to take all the stories one step further than the basic details you find on the internet and in many other books. I decided I would personally interview everyone involved in these stories. This is the result of my efforts, and I am sure that this book will be a treasure trove of paranormal information and hopefully will be an enjoyable read for everyone that reads it. I always state that all stories are alleged and are words from the witnesses themselves and not the words of the writer. I do not say any stories or interviews are true or false; I only started this interview project as a way for others to tell their own personal stories. Being somewhat of a skeptic, I write these stories from what I am told.

One thing I ask is that paranormal investigators get all the needed permission before entering any location in this book. E. Byrd nor The Oddporium, The Gallery of the Peculiar and the Bizarre cannot be held responsible for any damage or trespassing that could take place. **<u>Please Be Responsible And Ask Permission.</u>** Many of my interviews have links to websites where you can ask permission to visit locations mentioned.

E. Byrd, Author

Other Books Available

"What the Hell was That" ISBN-13: 978-1494869885

"Never Trust a $20 Motel." ISBN-13: 978-1494821869

"Legends and Lore of Clayton California" ISBN-13: 978-1523899630

"We Are The Gussethunters" ISBN-13: 978-1517145521

Books available through Amazon.com

About the Author

Born in Swindon, England and attending Kingsdown School, he made the move to the USA in 1986 and lived in London, Ohio.

When Byrd started his paranormal career in Ohio, he began by just visiting haunted locations and made the huge step from a paranormal investigator to a paranormal location promoter. He started with his first tour at the site of the famous Mothman sightings in Point Pleasant, West Virginia. And then followed by a permanent gig in Marysville Ohio at the site of a civil war doctor's house. One thing led to another, and within two years he was hosting eight permanent locations throughout Ohio. Byrd was starting to make a name for himself as being a promoter that only accepted the facts of the paranormal. He was not doing this to make a quick buck or offer false claims of other locations. He ended up moving to Northern California and working on "The Rock" at Alcatraz. Illness and the birth of his third child changed his path, and now he is a full-time college student and an author of a few popular paranormal books. Even though he has retired from the paranormal field, he can be seen at many para-cons or public speaking events throughout Northern California.

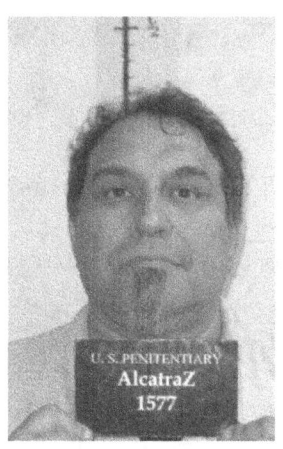

<u>Thanks to:</u>

Jenny Hosel; Corlis Byrd; Daniel Byrd; Amanda Byrd; Aiden Stanley; Lou Dimeri; Danny Reimer; Daren Olson; Ken Schuler; Beth Ann Busch; Richard H; TripAdvisor.com; New Castle Historical Society; Ed Richi; The Delaware Historical Society; http://history.delaware.gov; www.belmonthall.org;

In Memory of Barb and Leo Byrd, My Mum and Dad

xxx

Belmont Hall

This report was offered to me as a form of validation for this well-known story. I had found a paranormal member who did not want to share their name as they are a high ranking member of their local community. They told me over the phone that they had visited the historic Belmont Hall. *"Belmont Hall is a Georgian house located in Smyrna, Delaware, built around 1773 by Thomas Collins, who would become the eighth governor of Delaware... Collins was appointed a Lieutenant Colonel in Caesar Rodney's Upper Kent Militia in 1775 and promoted to Brigadier General in 1776 by General Washington. Collins garrisoned his property and built a stockade around the grounds. The balustrade and tower on the top of the house were erected at his direction and used as an observation post*

by sentries. As a member of the Assembly, Collins

agreed to raise a brigade of local militia which was

maintained primarily at his own expense while the war

lasted. Collins served with General George Washington

in New Jersey in 1777 but returned home to contend

with loyalist uprisings in Sussex County. He and his

militia most likely were involved in the efforts to block

General William Howell on his march from the Elk

River to the Battle of Brandywine. Belmont Hall is on

the Historic American Building Survey (HABS); is

marked by a State Historic Marker, a D.A.R. plaque and

is listed on The National Registry of Historic Places"

(www.belmonthall.org). The building is believed to be

haunted by the spirit of a guard who, during the

American Revolution, was shot and killed on the

building's Captain's Walk. Reports state his blood is still visible where he collapsed and died on the second floor. This not the case as the area has been cleaned over many years of occupancy.

The investigator I interviewed told me that during a daytime visit, he saw what he thought was an actor in uniform standing with his back to him, looking down a long hallway with no motion at all. Thinking nothing of this, the man continued to look around the room at the artwork and the furnishings. One more glance up still confirmed a re-enactor was standing thirty feet in front of this man. As the man walked towards the soldier, he was preparing to ask the man to move out of the doorway so he could pass. There had been no movement from this soldier the whole time my interviewee had seen him. The comment was made to me that it may have even been a mannequin standing there, as there was no movement at all. The man looked down so not to trip over a raised step that lied before him, and once his eyes returned to horizontal, the soldier was gone. In shock, the man rushed the last few steps to the doorway, and there was no sign of the soldier anywhere in the long hallway. If it was a man in a uniform, there was nowhere for him to run or hide. The soldier had vanished into thin air. On later investigation, it was reported this was the same area that the bloodstain is supposed to appear. Is this the entity that is reported by others? I feel this needs more investigation to collect more information.

Planning a visit? -

http://history.delaware.gov/museums/historic_sites.shtml

("There is certainly a world beyond our normal consciousness from which neither space nor time divides us, but only the barrier of our sense-perceptions.... this threshold is not immovable." ~William F. Barrett, On the Threshold of the Unseen, 1918)

Brick Hotel On The Circle

This former nineteenth-century hotel was formerly a public house and was associated with a rough crowd in the old days. The building has a lot of history. *"Originally known during the Civil War era as The Union Hotel... The existing structure was built in 1836. The first innkeeper was a gentleman by the name of Burton C. Baker, and history tells us that he was personally responsible for making the Brick Hotel one of the most popular hostelries on the Delmarva Peninsula. Apparently, it was a favorite lounging spot for staunch supporters of the Union. Southern sympathizers spent evenings in the barroom of the Eagle Hotel elsewhere on the Town Square and Circle. Apparently, the two factions engaged in some pretty interesting drunken brawls in the center of town! We also understand that throughout the years, it served as an informal club for the Delaware Bar as the courts moved from county to county"*

(http://www.thebrickhotel.com/history.php). Maybe this friction has caused a fair amount of paranormal activity in later years? Richard H. did not want to say anything about his encounter, but I was referred to a Tripadvisor post he had placed in 2015. It reads like this...

"This is a very haunted hotel, for certain."

Reviewed September 5, 2015

I had 5 encounters with ghosts there, and I didn't believe in them until now. In room 201, a woman was spotted. In room 202, I was awakened by my doorknob jiggling and turning and the door making a sound as if being pushed against. Then I heard some sobbing. It happened a second time at 4am, without the sobbing. They don't keep the doors closed there, so no air-pressure change was possible between the room and hallway.

My room key was under the bed. I always keep keys in my pants pocket in case I have to run for work. One sandal was also missing. I always take off my sandals and drop my shorts on top of the sandals, so I know where everything is. The other sandal was finally found on the other side of the room.

This morning in room 205, the shower turned suddenly cold. I turned around to see that the knob had moved 110 degrees and was a bit upset, enough not to spend the rest of my stay there.

But it's filled with history and had it not been for

the strange activity there, I would have loved it. It's old and needs work as all old places do, but I have a penchant for history and wanted to remain. It's a beautiful place and was built in 1705. I'm actually a descendant of Nathanael Greene who stayed there. But the ghost is definitely a prankster, and such things usually only get worse with time.

Room Tip: *Um, choose a different hotel unless you want the bejesus scared out of you.* " (TripAdvisor.com)

Thinking about an overnight stay or great food and drink? Please check out: http://www.thebrickhotel.com for more details.

("The spirits of the dead hallow a house, for me." ~Mark Twain, 1909)

Family Members Demise

This interview comes from Danny Reimer, investigator, and founder of D.R.O.P. (Delaware Researchers of the Paranormal). When I spoke to Danny, he offered a story about a house in Chester Heights, Pennsylvania. Danny's cousin lived in the house with his mother. The house always had a negative feeling, and family members appeared to be on edge most of the time.

One day while Danny was relaxing at home, he received a call from a frantic family member screaming through the phone. Once Danny had calmed the lady down on the other end of the line, he found out that his cousin had passed away in his bedroom a short time earlier. Immediately, Danny loaded up his car and headed over to his aunt's house and the scene of the demise.

Much later after the police and coroner had released the home to the family, Danny was asked to enter the home and help clean out his cousin's personal property from the bathroom and the bedroom. Entering the bathroom with a large trash bag in hand, he started opening cabinets and removing magazines, medications and other items that once belonged to his cousin. Danny opened up the mirror cabinet above the sink and removed all the bottles and other containers, he then tossed them all in the large black bag, making sure nothing was left behind. Once all the items were removed, he swung the glass door closed. This was when he saw the image of his recently deceased cousin in the mirror, just over his right shoulder. As Danny focused on the image that stood behind him, the entity stepped backward, turned and walked out of sight. Spinning around to try and witness the spirit that was just seen in the mirror, Danny darted to the door and peered down the hallway. There was no-one there, but in the opposite direction stood another family friend. The look on the face of the other man was that of shock, and with a shaky voice, he asked if anyone else saw what he just saw? Danny spoke up right away and said he just witnessed his dead cousin in the bathroom mirror. The other man said that he was entering the room and saw the same entity looking into that same bathroom Danny was standing. He then said that the image moved down the hall and disappeared in a blurry haze. Both men hurried down the hallway and looked in towards the bedrooms, but there was no sign of the entity that had just shown itself. The description offered to me was that of a young man with a very sad expression on his face, but the entity appeared fully intact and not translucent as many other spirits have appeared in other stories in the past. Calling out from the center of the hallway, Danny said to what he thought was his dead cousin," Was it really that bad?", expressing the concern for his unexpected passing. There were no audible voices, but right at that moment, there was the sound of objects moving in another room. Items striking the walls where the death had taken place. With super fast reactions, Danny darted into the bedroom, only to see nothing at all. The room was bare and baron and all evidence of the death had been removed earlier that day. Four bare walls confronted Danny, but he knows what he heard was clearly items slamming in the room. Just in case he could have been mistaken, Danny started checking all the other rooms in the home, but there was no sign of any objects damages or laying on the floor. The friend then turned to Danny and asked who and what was that? The response came clear and forthright. "It was Eddie, my cousin, and he was here to tell us something important."

The activity had forced the friend to leave the house for the night. Danny also thought it was time to lock up the house and return to his family. Still not fully believing what was witnessed that day, he turned the key in the lock and walked back to the car. Climbing in the car and sliding on his seat belt, he takes one final glimpse at the house and pulls out of the driveway.

Time passes by, and life moves ahead as normal. Danny returns to his place of employment, and the aunt is back in the home when one day Danny gets another call from a familiar number. The aunt is wondering if he could bring his paranormal group out to look over the house. The aunt had expressed small things were happening that she was unable to explain and was looking for validation of sorts. Danny asked what sort of activity she was experiencing and how he could help her. She said that she would lay her keys on the table and leave the room, but upon her return, the keys were gone. She would search for the keys and finally find them in the refrigerator or inside of a cabinet. She said that she would be sitting alone in the house and the shower would turn on, and the water would run until she enters the bathroom and turns off the flow of water herself. She did mention that the handle to the shower was rather stiff and hard to operate and she sometimes had a problem twisting the handle to stop the rushing water. She could not imagine the handle slipping to the open position on its own. But the thing that would scare her the most was witnessing the door handle to Eddie's room turn, and the door would fly open. And to make things worse, the door would sometimes close and latch itself as if operated by a human hand, but no hand was seen. As an afterthought, she mentioned the sounds of pots and pans moving in the kitchen, but when entering the kitchen, nothing was seen to be out of place.

Danny had a thought that all this new activity was either Eddie making his presence known or a form of Poltergeist that was responsible for all the missing items throughout the house. Danny suggested that he bring in a few friends to help him investigate the house. The Aunt was content with this reply and invited them over. This group of friends were made up of Kayla Kemp, Amanda Fabi and Rachel Kenney, all members of Danny's paranormal team and all close friends. When the group arrived at the house, the group members expressed the feeling in the home as being light and airy, where the basement and attic are dark and foreboding. The investigation was under way and all evidence was documented as the group moved room to room. After reviewing the notes from the investigation, Danny reported to me that the house had a steady 73 degrees temperature and nothing seemed out of place. The electronic readings were average, and there were no hot spots at all in this house. As night fell, I was told that the group took up residence in the living room and did what I used to call "quiet time." This is a period of at least five minutes when no one talks and everyone listens. The only communication is made with hand gestures and head nods, very much like fighters in a combat zone. It was during this time the group experienced what was said to have been whispering from the kitchen area. The group all heard what sounded like a male's voice coming from the adjacent room and all the members were excited to listen to the EVPs *(electronic voice phenomena (EVP) are sounds found on electronic recordings that are interpreted as spirit voices that have been either unintentionally recorded or intentionally requested and recorded).* To their disbelief, when they played back the recording, they heard no voices at all, only the ticking from the clock on

27

the wall. The only other sound was that of the people of the house shuffling in their seats. Slightly dishearten by not finding any proof from the kitchen, the group made their way up the stairs to the attic space. Once entering the darkened room through a narrow doorway, the group once more take their positions in the form of a circle and turn on their electronic devices. After a few minutes of silence, Danny decided it was time to get answers to a series of questions he had in mind. Slowly, and in a firm but not forceful voice, he asked the following question. "Did you mean to hurt yourself ?" Then there was a period of silence as the temperature of the room started to drop in a drastic manner. The recorder was then played back right away once the room turned bitter cold. To the amazement of the group, a voice came back after the initial question was asked with a clear "NO." After hearing this answer, the next question was asked: " Did someone make you do it?" There was no reply to this question, but there was a definite change in the feeling and atmosphere of the room. All members of the group started to find it hard to breathe; as if they were under water, and the struggle to catch their breath was ongoing. It was at that point that Danny and his fellow investigators turned towards the stairs and then descended to the kitchen once more. Once each member passed through the narrow doorway, their breathing returned to normal and no one had any breathing issues. This was when he snapped a series of photographs down the hallway as he sat on the stairs. It was then when he observed a solid ball of light moving across the floor. Jumping to his feet, Danny slowly followed the ball of light that skipped across the hardwood floors only to be confronted by a black shadow that stood in the hallway in front of him. Danny was somewhat scared by what he was confronted with, as this dark image in the dark hallway was holding what appeared to be a shotgun. This was enough for even the most seasoned investigator to raise their blood pressure and increase their heart rate. The shotgun image vanished as quickly as it appeared and the remaining time consisted of no activity at all throughout the house. The group decided to leave the house and review all the evidence collected from the previous hours investigation. As they wrapped up all the equipment and were preparing to leave the property, they heard what sounded like the slamming of drawers in the bathroom. The house was starting to take on a mind of its own at this point. The recorders were instantly turned back on and left to record while they

30

finished packing up their last few pieces of equipment. As they prepared to exit, Danny asked if Eddie was there, and after a minute of silence, the recorders were shut off for one final time and placed in their carrier. When the crew were traveling home, one of the members rewound the recorder to hear no response from Eddie at all, nothing but silence.

So you expect this is the end of this story with details of a haunting of a family member's home, but that is where you are wrong. The evidence does point more towards the cousin Eddie, but after a lot of documentation review, it was concluded that over 15 people have died on the property over the years. The land was once the site for a school that caught fire and killed about 7 children. This is in addition to the normal amount of family members passing and the occasional incident that may have happened in the back yard. With this new-found information, the group had planned to return and see if there was a connection between the unexplained sadness of the attic and the basement that was present before Eddie killed himself.

With permission from the Aunt, the group reassembled at the house and for yet another time, set up all their equipment and preparing for what was a new chapter in this investigation. The audio equipment was set up, and then a new set of questions were ready to be posed to the deceased. This time the focus was on the children and other people that had died around the area of the home, with little attention drawn towards Eddie. Danny and his crew started the questioning with the normal, "Is there anyone who would like to speak with us tonight?" There was no response to this questioning, so the group had thought they had hit a brick wall and that it may be a quiet night for them all. Moving from room to room, there was no paranormal activity at all stirring in the house. This was starting to look like an early exit for the group until noises were heard coming from an adjacent room. Immediately the voice recorder was turned on, and the record button was triggered. There was only one question asked at that point, "Who is there?" When the recording was played back, they heard in a foggy, hazy voice state two names, "Stephanie and Eddie." This was an awakening for Danny, as he knew who Stephanie was. She had died from a drug overdose and was a former girlfriend of Eddie.

There was always a concern that both of these deceased were turned on to hardcore drugs by an unknown person. It must have been a friend of both Eddie and Stephanie who started this road to destruction, but the person was never revealed or spoken of during these two's earthbound life. This was an opportunity to find out who caused the two to die prematurely. This had gone from a normal paranormal investigation to a (of sorts) homicide investigation. Danny's family have a strong background in law enforcement and knew the right things to ask. Sitting quietly in a darkened room, Danny started to try and find out more details and reasoning behind the deaths of these two former sweethearts.

Sadness came across Danny and other members

of the group, when there is no evidence revealed or voices explaining the third member of this drug circle. It is the impression of the family that there was a third person involved and that person was a drug addict who was killed in a suspicious motorcycle accident a short period after the others had passed. Some people wanted to know the name of the person that was there when Eddie killed himself and the ex-girlfriend overdosed a short time later. In both cases, there were signs of another person present just before both took their last breaths.

With the group left bewildered and somewhat lost, next came yet another shock to the people involved in this night's investigation. It was the audible sound of counting, "1,2,3,4......," then an outburst of children laughing. Taken aback by this sudden change in activity, the group was forced to put on hold the murder / suicide questioning and turn to a more jovial interaction with what sounded like children enjoying a simple counting game. The use of counting and nursery rhymes were heard floating throughout the room. There was a positive interaction during this short period, even as far as the investigators knocking on one wall and getting responses tapped on a different wall. At a point during the investigation, one of the ladies from the group said she witnessed a school girl standing in a corner of the room, only to vanish within a split second. There was no form of voice communication, but what you thought could be residual, was actually high quality interaction taking place. The night ended with a long period of inactivity and no sign of any more paranormal evidence, so the group packed up and shipped out, while all the time discussing all the excitement that that night had brought them.

Since this last documented activity had taken place, the home has since been sold, and a new family has moved in. Danny has lost touch with all the activity that may be going on in this home, but he did express to me that if he ever got the call to investigate once more, he would do it without hesitation. To the day of this book being completed, there is still no proof that there was a person with Eddie or Stephanie when they died, even though there is so much evidence pointing that way. We may never know who the third person was, or if it was in fact the victim of the bike accident. Could the spirit of the friend / dealer still be intimidating Eddie and Stephanie from beyond the grave? Did Eddie try to communicate and tell the name of that person, but was stopped when questioned on voice recording? We may never know, but what we do know is that the tortured spirit of two young people whose lives were ruined by drugs are still wanting to tell their story. If they are able to find justice, they may be able to rest in peace and maybe break the bond of bullying from the afterlife.

("He stood looking after them... as though he had perceived that they had come back accompanied by a ghost a-piece." ~Charles Dickens, Little Dorrit)

Hospital Guardian

Lou Dimeri, a docent and radio host, was working at the McKeesport Hospital near Pittsburgh, PA, as a security officer for a well-known company. His job duties consisted of many different tasks, but one of the more unusual tasks was to escort the remains of patients who had passed while still in the hospital's care. After an official time of death was documented, the bodies would be placed in the morgue for collection from the immediate family members. But in the Jewish religion, there is a practice called The *"chevra kadisha."* The *chevra kadisha* dictates that is a Jewish burial society which usually consists of volunteers, men, and women, who prepare the deceased for proper Jewish burial. Their job is to ensure that the body of the deceased is shown proper respect, ritually cleansed, and shrouded. Someone is assigned to sit with the body until family members are present to claim the body.

This was not the first time Lou was asked to do the duty of watching over the body, so he had a good idea what he was supposed to do. The call was received, and Lou and a fellow guard started to head down towards the basement where the body was laid out in a respectful manner. Both men responded to the call, but only Lou was the selected one to watch over the body. The men made their way down the busy hallways of the main hospital floors and pressed the button on the elevator, stood back and waited for the doors to open. Their attention was jarred away from the hustle and bustle of the hospital floor by the sharp ping of the elevator reaching their selected point. The elevator doors opened, and both men step in and away from the consent buzz of a hospital ward. The sound of mellow music played in their heads as the elevator drops towards the lower floors of the building. With the sound of a small bell and a sudden jarring halt, the doors open up, and the sight of concrete walls and the hum of a generator was the only thing to welcome them to this contrast to the busy, well-lit hospital ward. As both men step out of the elevator, they feel the coldness of the dark hallways that faced them and the echo of their heavy boots on the concrete resonating down the long hallway. The men make the right hand turn to yet another narrow passageway. This passageway was poorly lit with only the light from the morgue shining through the large glass window which is used for the

41

viewing of the bodies. On the opposite wall were two other doors that lead to the bathrooms. As the men made their way to the door that entered the morgue, both men peek in through the window, only to see a man sat with his back to them and the door.

The description of this man was that of an elderly gentleman with long gray hair and an ill-fitting gray suit. Offering this man some respect, the two officers did not push on the door and enter. It was clear to both men that a member of the church had already arrived without the notification of the two security officers. Both men turned and started to walk back to the elevator, the whole time wondering how someone could have made it to the morgue so quickly. The second officer pulled out his radio and told the front desk that there was already a man watching over the body and they were going to return to the main floor of the hospital and await their next assignment. The front desk radioed back and said that they did not know who was down there with the corpse, as the family had not yet been notified and this was the only death reported that day. This was a severe breach of security to allow a stranger to be in the morgue alone, let alone making it to restricted parts of the hospital. So Lou and the fellow officer turned tail and quickly headed back to the room where the intruder was seen sitting not moments before. Without even looking, the men burst into the morgue only to find the body on a gurney covered in a white sheet and an empty chair pulled out from the wall. Both men reacted in a surprised manner. They looked at each other, and without a word, they started to look around the small room. There was no one living in the room except for the two flustered guards. The next instinct was to check the only other place anyone could be in this basement; the bathrooms. One man entered the men's room, and the other entered the women bathroom. After all stalls were checked, Lou exited the bathroom expecting his partner to walk out with the man in the gray suit, but to his amazement, the other officer came out empty handed. Both men were once again in a state of shock as it was now evident that the man who was watching over the corpse had disappeared into thin air. There was no way this man could have left the room and made it to the elevator without passing the two officers. He was witnessed by two men and then within one minute, he was gone.

Later that night the family came to claim the body and a member of the church showed up to watch over the remains, taking the place of what was a haunting spirit that was seen earlier that night.

("We don't believe in ghosts, Mrs. Phipps."

"Don't matter if you believe in them or not. If they're there, they're there."

~Joan Lowery Nixon, The Haunting)

McKeesport Electrical Problem

Continuing the haunting stories of McKeesport Hospital, we now move on to another occurrence that happened on Halloween night many years ago. Lou Dimeri was on duty in his security guard role when he received a call from the head nurse. The head nurse was a disliked individual who made her staff members feel uncomfortable while on their shift. This was a very large rotund lady who did not stand for any tomfoolery during the working hours. It was all business, all the time with her, and it showed by her actions towards others under her command. The head nurse said that even though they were not supposed to be at this location, two of her staff members had ventured to the 6th floor to observe the construction that was going on. They had reported back that all the room call buttons were flashing on and off and the telephone was ringing. There was no staff working up there and no patients, only construction workers who were stripping the entire ward clean of all items before demolition started. It had been made clear to all staff members of the hospital that floor 6 was off limits to everyone except the construction workers and the security guards.

Lou was summoned to the head nurses office for more details on what was happening on floor 6. Knocking on the door, he was called in with a rough voice and told to take a seat as she pointed to a chair and never lifted her face to acknowledge his pressance. Feeling uncomfortable in the presence of this overbearing large woman, Lou proceeded to receive a briefing of all the activity that had supposed to have taken place during the two nurses trip to the forbidden floor. Taking out his notebook, Lou only wrote down two lines, "Call buttons" and the word "telephone." Lou excused himself and left the office, grabbing his flashlight on the way out.

Heading towards the elevator, Lou entered the elevator and pushed the number 6 button on the panel. The elevator surged in an upward motion while the number display started to count up from 1 to 6. Once the elevator display showed floor 6, the ride came to a halt, and the doors pulled open. Stepping out onto a very quiet landing, Lou made his way to a set of solid doors that led to the ward that was being remodeled. Stepping on pieces of debris from the construction site, Lou made his way to the doors. Pushing firmly on the doors, they swung open to reveal a very dark and cold area with lots of construction equipment laying on the floor and remains of drywall panels scattered throughout the area. It was so dark in the room that Lou had to turn on the flashlight to look down the extent of the long ward towards the far wall that was a fair distance away. The two nurses had reported the lights flashing on all the walls next to the doorways to what was once the hospital private rooms. Lou saw nothing out of the ordinary, the whole place was silent, and there was nothing happening at all. The ward was still and motionless, and it appeared that this was a Halloween prank that was played by the two nurse supervisors who had reportedly ascended to the 6th floor.

Seeing the 6th floor was as quiet as a church mouse, Lou backed out of the ward and pulled the doors closed behind himself. Walking back to the elevator, tripping and stumbling over drywall chips, Lou would find himself believing a prank had been pulled on the head nurse and himself, and the head nurse would not take the prank lightly, and now it was Lou's place to tell her. Descending in the elevator, Lou braced himself for the meeting with the head nurse. He was more fearful of what he had to tell her than any other scary experience he had to deal with during his tenure as a security officer at this location. Exiting the elevator and taking what seemed like the very long walk to the head nurses office, he knocks on the door and waits for permission to enter. A loud roar comes from the other side of the office door and taking a seat once more, Lou expressed that there was no flashing lights and no telephone ringing on the 6th floor. In fact, the telephone line was disconnected and not in service at all. He even expressed there was no power to the ward to allow the lights to flash. Power was run to the location by extension power cords from another floor. After he had made his report, he then left the office and made his way back to his post, but prior to him leaving, the head nurse expressed that she personally would go up and take a look around the 6th floor and familiarize herself with the situation before disciplining her two nurse supervisors.

Time passed by on that Halloween night and the normal amount of drunks with injuries; and many in costume, had made their way into the emergency room and were admitted for many different complaints. Later that night Lou received another call, once more it was the head nurse. This time the overpowering woman came across in a very disturbed and nervous manner. Lou was told to report to the 6th floor once more, this time he was to take the maintenance man with him, as there were reports of the call lights flashing. The call was made to the maintenance man who was named "Browning." Browning agreed to accompany Lou back up to the 6th floor of the Shaw Building once more. Once again, Lou followed the same steps he had taken earlier in the evening, but this time he was not alone. Stepping onto the elevator, pressing number 6 on the panel and making their way up to the abandoned floor. The elevator doors pulled open once more, and both men made their way to the large double doors. The area was very quiet and no sound was heard coming from the closed ward. Pushing open the doors both men were shocked to witness all the call lights flashing on and off. What was once a very dark hallway, was now lit up like a Christmas tree. All the call lights were flashing on the main desk board. Lou asked where the power box would be as it was evident that there was a short of some sort which caused the lights to flash like that. Both men made their way to a large steel box that was mounted on the wall in a small side room that was once used as a janitor's closet. Browning reaches up and tugs hard on the steel door, causing a huge noise as the rusty hinges gave way under the pressure. To the utter horror of both men, they witnessed no wiring at all within the box. The wires had all been removed from the entire 6th floor. All the breakers were scattered on the floor, and there was no copper wiring anywhere to be seen. There was no electricity on that floor at all.

Lou turned to speak with Browning, but Browning had high tailed out of there and all Lou saw was the large doors slamming shut behind Browning's hasty departure. Now Lou was alone with the lights continuing to flash. He thought this could be a prank being played on him, so he moved towards the switchboard that sat on a now abandoned desk. Looking down at the series of lights, he was then startled when the phone rang. Looking at the switchboard, there were no cords connecting it to any form of electricity or phone line. It sat alone on the table-top, covered in a thick layer of drywall dust, so much so that anyone could have grabbed the phone and walked off with it without having to unplug any wiring.

Not sure what to do next, Lou tentatively reached down and picked up the receiver of the phone and brought it to his ear. Not saying a word, he heard a strange hissing coming from the phone. It sounded like "white noise, " but there may have been a few distant words mixed in with the static. Causing alarm, Lou dropped the phone and made a quick exit himself towards the exit but stopped at the elevator on the other side of the double doors. Knowing there was no electricity and power at all on that floor, it was hard to explain where the electricity came from to operate the phone and the switchboard. Once again, Lou built up the courage to peek inside the double doors once more. Taking a deep breath, he pushed open one of the doors, only to see total darkness and complete silence greeting his eyes and ears.

A formal report was required regarding the incident, and once it was submitted, Lou received yet another call. This time it was to meet with his security group superior. Once Lou had taken his seat, he was informed that writing fake incident reports were grounds for termination and he was on thin ice due to his Halloween prank. Lou tried to explain that he was not the only one to witness this incident and that he can find at least four others that had experienced the same occurrence. After a few phone calls, Lou was told that his report was verified and he was free to return to his duties. Other reports of strange goings on have been reported on the same floor after its renovation and remodel. What is causing this disturbance is still unknown. *("At first cock-crow, The ghosts must go, Back to their quiet graves below." ~Theodosia Garrison, "The Neighbors")*

Strange Occurrence at Rockwood Mansion

The tours that pass through New Castle County DE. and in particular Rockwood mansion, are becoming more popular by leaps and bounds. This is partly due to Louis and Phil who have been hosting ghost hunts since they started to offer them. Phil is an older gentleman and dresses in the style of the Edwardian times, while Louis sports his famous top hat and tails for the events. Both Louis and Phil appear to be suited to this old mansion of the Delaware wealthy, from the end of the 1800's. I would not be surprised if many visitors look up as they make their way up the driveway and see these two gentlemen looking out of the windows on a dark evening. Guests would surely feel they have seen ghosts even before entering the property.

On this one night, there was a small group of people who had come out to take the evening tour. Within this small group was a very old lady who appeared to be doubled over from old age and she could barely walk. She hobbled around on a 4 pronged walking frame and would take only a few steps before having to stop to catch her breath.

Louis and Phil had three volunteers helping them that night, and it was very obvious that this little old lady that they thought may have been in her 90's, would not be fit enough to take an extended walking tour of this vast location. The house is very large and houses many staircases and steps throughout. The staff congregated and discussed a polite way of telling this old lady that she would not be able to take the tour due to her inability to walk and climb stairs. It was decided that they would allow her to stay on the ground floor of the building and look around with the help of one of the volunteers. Louis expressed the concern and offered the aforementioned plan to her. This way she could still get a feel for the location and not leave disappointed that she had missed out on an educational evening out. After taking a seat, she said that ever since she was a young girl, she had always wanted to come and visit the mansion, but had never had the opportunity prior to this one day. She almost begged Louis to allow her to take the tour. She said that she was getting close to death and had finally been able to tour the house she remembered from her childhood, over 80 years before.

The kindheartedness of Louis said that they

would assign a volunteer to her and help her get around the facility. She smiled and agreed to this arrangement.

Time passes by, and the tour is ready to start. Introductions and rules were laid out for the guests, and everyone started to move out of the room. Louis looks around the room to confirm all the guests had moved out, only to see one of his guides holding his back. This was a fit and active young fellow and had never had any issues touring the mansion before, but this night he started to feel pain in his lower back. Another guide overheard this conversation and came over and expressed the same feeling of discomfort in the same area of their back. This appeared to be an unusual coincidence, but what made this even more unusual was the fact that the old lady that was doubled over with her cane was now walking in an upright stance. She was seen at the end of the hall standing tall and appearing in great spirits.

The pain continued to grow in the two young volunteers, but the old lady started to appear to be walking at a normal casual pace. Lou witnessed the moment when one of the volunteers could not stand the pain anymore and had to take a seat half way through the tour. It was not long after that the second volunteer was unable to complete the tour either. Both were now sat on chairs grimacing in pain. It was at that point Louis catches a glance of the old lady, who was now bounding up the stairs with her cane under her arm. The cane was now useless as if there was never a need for it. The lady stood tall and proud and kept up a sprightly pace. The whole time Louis kept an eye on this lady, and he was amazed by the transformation from the withered old lady who was doubled over in pain that entered the front door and the active for her age lady who had no trouble climbing all the stairs throughout the tour.

Within an hour or so the tour comes to an end, and everyone was now standing back in the same room from where they had started. The crowd moved in and the last person to enter the room was the old lady who was now escorted by the two volunteers. Louis and Phil say their goodbyes and the crowd disperses. As everyone starts to leave, Louis noticed that the old lady was now using her cane again. She appeared to have resorted back to the stooped position, and by the time she had taken a few steps out into the dark Delaware air, she was back to the very old frail lady who only had a few weeks to live. She moved slowly and would stop every few steps for a breath of the crisp cool air. She started to shuffle her feet and needed assistance from fellow tourists to make it to the parking lot. It was at this same time that both of the volunteers seemed to have a complete recovery from their ailments, with both of them feeling no pain or stiffness in their joints or bones. Their recovery was that of someone that had never had back problems ever before. Both were surprised and could not explain what had just happened to them. Both expressing the feeling of being very old and unable to walk without a form of support. All the staff members had noticed the old lady walking briskly throughout the tour as if she was young once more. Most people put it down to adrenaline but a few felt it was something more than excitement from a ailing female.

Could this have been some form of paranormal activity to where whoever haunts the house wanted this little old lady to take the tour she had been wanting to do all her life or was this just adrenaline kicking in and the weather getting to the pair of spritely volunteers? Louis expressed this is one of the more unusual stories he can share about the location he has grown to love.

Plan a visit? - go to http://nccde.org/431/Rockwood-Park-Museum for more details.

(*"Some places speak distinctly. Certain dark gardens cry aloud for a murder; certain old houses demand to be haunted; certain coasts are set apart for shipwreck." ~Robert Louis Stevenson)*

Wanda's Little British Friend

Wanda Theresa is a hometown girl from Bear, DE. Wanda was an empath from birth and had inherited these abilities from her mother, while also passing the ability on to her children. "Empathy is the ability to read and understand people and be in-tune with or resonate with others, voluntarily or involuntarily of one's empath capacity. *Empaths have the ability to scan others psyche for thoughts and feelings or for past, present, and future life occurrences. Many empaths are unaware of how this actually works, and have long accepted that they were sensitive to others."*

http://healing.about.com/cs/empathic/a/uc_empathtraits. htm

Coming from a strict catholic background, the ability to interact with spirits and other forms of paranormal was frowned upon by the church. So the feelings had to be suppressed and not spoken of for most of her childhood and adolescence years. The feelings were forcefully ignored for many years, but when she started to mature, she started to read about these abilities she knew she possessed. After many trips to the library and other locations with documents explaining the feelings Wanda had experienced for so many years, she made the decision to visit one of the more reliable physics in the Wilmington DE. area to try and help her answer the questions that had plagued her for most of her early years.

The day came when Wanda had to visit the

physic for her appointment, and her nerves were all over the place as she was not sure what to expect. Once she walked in and took a seat, the physic asked her what she wanted to learn? Her response was that of needing to know how to use her skills in a more productive manner. The physic kicked back in her chair and remained silent for a few moments, then; leaning forward from her relaxed posture, she said that Wanda did not need any help from her as she already had the skills and did not need her help. It was decided that Wanda would become an understudy to the physic and learn how to use her skills to help others.

After a period of time, Wanda had become confident with her new-found abilities and was not afraid of any form of interaction with the spirit world at all. When I asked her what it is like to receive messages from the dead, she explained to me that messages come in the form of images and cryptic signs. It was then she would translate the images to make sense of what was being relayed to her.

So when I asked for an interview, I asked of a very special moment in her paranormal career that would be classed as a life changing experience. This was that experience that left Wanda astonished and dumbfounded by her abilities.

After forming a paranormal group with a few of her close friends and while building a portfolio of locations investigated, she received a phone call from a gentleman named Owen. He expressed interest in having Wanda and her paranormal group come to three of his businesses that all appeared to have some form of paranormal activity. After collecting as much information as possible over the phone, a date was set, and Wanda called her team to arms. The group had done many investigations prior to this trip, and this one seemed just like many of the others. Of the three locations that all butted up side by side on this busy street, the location with the most activity was that of a hair salon that sat between the owner's two other businesses. The people that worked in the salon had reported the sightings of a little girl inside the establishment. The first report was made a while back when Owen was locking up the facility. The workday had finally come to an end, and everyone had left with the exception of Owen. After making sure everything was turned off, and the building was secure, he flicked off the lights located next to the front door. Pulling the door closed and with a twist of his wrist, he turned the key. He wiggled the handle to make sure the lock was soundly in place. Satisfied all was secured, he turned away and proceeded towards his car that sat not more than 20 feet away from the store front. As he approached the vehicle, he had the strong urge to turn around and look at the shop once more. This was not a normal thing for him to do, but the desire was so strong, he turned on his heels and glanced back. To his amazement, he saw a young child standing in the window frame peering out towards him. The account states that this image then turned and disappeared into the darkness of the salon. With a rush of fear that he had locked up the building leaving a child in the bathroom, he hustled back to the store. Fumbling for his keys, he quickly unlocked the door and stepped inside. He called

out but heard no response. He made it clear in a gentler

voice that he was sorry he had locked her in, and she

must leave immediately. He flipped on the lights and

started to wander the premise, calling out to the little girl

the whole time. He scanned all levels of the building,

and it was then made clear that there was no one on the

premise. Not sure what to think, Owen shook his head

and put the vision down to many long hours working the

salon with very little rest.

Bright and early the next morning, he asked the

staff if they had ever experienced any form of ghostly

activity in any of the three buildings? Many of the staff

said they had not, but a few mentioned they think they

had witnessed a person sitting in the third chair in the

salon, but every time they would turn to look, there was nothing or no-one there to see. Every time the staff thought they were seeing things and considered their daily duties to be over taxing and the images were a figment of their imagination.

Once the paranormal team arrived after the salon had closed for the night, Owen was there waiting. The ladies of the paranormal group normally will do a walk through, which consists of requested information and locations of electric outlets for equipment and other hazards that may lurk in the deep dark depths of these 1700's brick and stone buildings. After the walk through was completed, Wanda and her co-founder Dolly Ziegler set about setting up cameras and other forms of paranormal equipment throughout the hot spots of activity that had been reported. One of the main areas of sightings was a salon chair where all the staff had witnessed the apparition. Dolly and her fellow Delaware City Ghost Hunters prepared all the gadgets for the investigation when they started to hear a gentle chuckle and giggling coming from behind them. All the members turned to see Wanda sitting in the infamous third chair, and sporting a strange look on her face. Then the group heard more giggling coming from their leader, but what made this seem out of the ordinary was the fact the laughing was not that of Wanda. Wanda is an adult lady with children of her own, but this voice coming out of her was that of a five-year-old girl. Everyone in the room dropped what they were doing and descended on the area Wanda was sitting. The voice coming out of Wanda was not that of an American but more British in nature. The voices coming out of Wanda then started to offer a few snippets of personal information, which had not been revealed or even known till that point in time. The little voice claimed her name was Mary Beth and she was a happy child. She also said that she was happy to meet them all that night. It was then that Wanda rose from her chair and started to shake out her arms as if to break free from something that was clinging to her. Then the normal voice of Wanda returned as she told the spirit to leave her body. The whole time this voice was coming out of Wanda, she was in full consciousness, but she had no control over her words, tone or expressions. Once the voices had stopped and Wanda moved to another seat, she felt mentally drained and a little scared, as this had never happened to her before. The feeling of listening to a voice that is resonating in your skull but is not your voice must be terrifying. The group converged on the area and attempted to help the spirit in any way they could.

After the investigation, it was discovered that an old barn once stood on the site and burnt down in a fire in the 1700's and the area was also very active in the "underground railroad."

Two weeks later Delaware City Ghost Hunters returned to the salon and were told there was no more activity in that salon since they left that night. This was Wanda's first experience at channeling, and it came out of the blue with no warning at all. She was not prepared for it, and it scared her slightly, but now she is very much prepared for it to happen again. As of the time of the interview, it had only happened that one time.

Wanda and Dolly are still active with Delaware City Ghost Hunters and still offer free services to anyone contacting them.

("A person terrified with the imagination of specters, is more reasonable than one who thinks the appearance of spirits fabulous and groundless." ~Joseph Addison)

Shadow on the Driveway

To return to yet another tale of the unusual from the Rockwood Mansion, we meet Louis Dimeri once more. As he normally does, he meets the guests at the front door and then would usher them into the meeting room. While standing in the doorway on a cool October night, the lights from the 10 feet high decorative lamps light the driveway in a romantic manner. Louis and his helper Rachael stepped out of the doorway and walked into the courtyard. Just wasting time, they both wandered back and forth while making idle chit-chat. It was at this moment Rachael was stopped in her tracks and in mid sentence she stammered her words. Her eyes slowly got larger and larger as she was clearly focusing on something that had caught her eye. Louis quickly turned in the same direction that she was looking and to his amazement, he witnessed a shadow that was cast from one of the lamp poles. Louis continued to focus on the shadow but called out to Rachael and asked her to explain what she was seeing. Without diverting their eyes, she responded that she sees what would normally be a shadow cast by a person that would be standing under a lamp post. The only setback to this description was the fact that there was no-one standing under the lamp. As both the guides stared at the shadow that was cast on the ground, the shadow started to move down the driveway. The shadow would start to fade as the intensity of the one lamp would start to dim, and then the shadow would start to build in density as the next lamp started to light the path. The pattern of motion continued the length of the driveway. Seeing Louis is a well-known ghost hunter in his area, he was obligated to head towards the moving shadow. Louis took the lead and Rachael followed close in his footsteps. When they reached the end of the lit driveway, Rachael had seen enough and insisted that they both return to the mansion and wait for the guests to show up in the safety of the stately home. Louis agreed and swiveled on the spot and started to pace his way back to the glow of the romantic mansion. Rachael had kept up the pace and stood very close to Louis, the whole time glancing over her shoulder to see if there were additional shadows beyond the two that they had cast themselves.

Once the couple felt comfortable that the paranormal occurrence had passed, both let down their guard. Relaxing and taking a few deep breaths and laughing off what had just happened. It was at that exact moment that the sound of horse hooves were heard coming up the driveway. Looking at each other, Louis states he had no idea anyone was taking a coach ride to the event that night, but he was very much looking forward to what this horse and carriage looked like as it appeared. The couple stood aside and waited for the horses to emerge from the tree lined entrance. The sound of hooves got louder and then came the smell of horse manure. The sound had become so loud that the brain expected to see the carriage right in front of them, but there was nothing but open space. The smell of horses and the sound of hooves were so clear that it was impossible to be a prank or any form of confusion with other sounds from surrounding areas. Once more this caused Rachael to start feeling uneasy and this made Louis excited that this second incident had happened within minutes of the shadow account. Shortly after this exciting encounter and once the guests started to show up, the driveway remained peaceful but has left its mark on both of the hosts.

("If, after I depart this vale, you ever remember me and have thought to please my ghost, forgive some sinner and wink your eye at some homely girl." ~H.L. Mencken)

Trip to Ohio.

Dr. Lou, radio show host on "Parallel Worlds," took a trip to visit me in Ohio after I had spent many years being a guest on numerous radio shows.

After a few years in the paranormal business, I invited Dr. Lou out to investigate many of my locations. This was also in co-ordination with another of "Parallel Worlds" regular guest, Cindy Riggs. Cindy is an internationally known Psychic, Spiritual Mentor, Universal Channel and Defrag-Mentor. The date was set, and Lou and Cindy confirmed the ability to make the date.

Lou had showed up first while Cindy was on a

delay, so I made sure we would get Lou a hotel room from one of my sponsors. The hotel had worked with me as a location for all the paranormal investigators to stay after their events. They checked in and found themselves on the top floor in the back of the building. These rooms were often used by staff or as "free rooms." Once both of us had settled in, we returned to a large warehouse in the center of the Central Ohio town. After a few minutes, Cindy made her appearance, and everyone hugged each other and shared a moment of joy that we finally got to meet each other in the flesh.

After the formalities had been completed, the daytime paranormal investigation began. Lou armed with his dousing rods, Cindy with her mind and myself operating the camera to document this once in a lifetime event. Cindy started with a protection prayer, and then we started a tour of the building to get the guests used to the many floors that make up the building. Once this was finished, Lou grabbed his rods, and I grabbed a handful of cameras and video cameras. The second floor was one of the floors that had offered the best evidence over the years, so the group made a beeline to that floor. Once the stairs were ascended, and everyone turned into a wide-open space, both of the visitors were driven to the front of the building. As they approached a window where it had been reported a doppelganger of myself had been seen on a few occasions, Cindy started to feel unsettled. She was being drawn to a tiny room with no windows. This room was the same room that a member of a well-known U.S. paranormal TV show, had once gone and started to be very disrespectful, and the same room he was physically tossed out of by what was called "a gargoyle looking creature." This so-called "hard man" of the paranormal, was in tears and shaking after this attack. I had not mentioned anything about this attack that had happened a month before, and I wanted to see if it was a real attack or just a hoax. Cindy's pace slowed as she approached the doorway, she started to feel hesitant to enter this tiny storage room. Lou had pulled out the rods, and he was asking questions at the entrance of the doorway. I was documenting the whole event on camera. Cindy started to move into the dark room and disappeared from sight of the others in the party. Without any warning, Cindy scurries out of the room, looks square in the camera and says " The scariest room ever." Please view this incident at https://www.youtube.com/watch?v=OVsPwF1pQRM,

Please note that neither of my guests knew where or what had happened in the building as I refused to tell them locations of known activity or happenings. Cindy finds herself approaching the elevator where an employee lost his life in a nasty decapitation incident. Once more, she had no idea what to expect. As she walked to one side of the elevator, she was immediately drawn to the other side of the elevator. She was then overcome by grief as she said this was the site of a horrible death. Lou was able to communicate that this was not an accident and that the man who was dead was killed for knowing "too much." Later that night, I allowed Lou to lead the paranormal tour, and with the help of the guests, they revealed lots of new details about a murder of a child and their involvement with organized crime in the area.

Cindy continues to live and work in Columbus, Ohio. You can contact her at www.cindyriggs.com. I highly recommend you speak with her if you are having negative paranormal activity bothering you. As stated before, she saved my life in the past, and I think of her as my hero. Lou still hosts tours at Rockwood Mansion in Delaware.

("I don't believe that ghosts are "spirits of the dead" because I don't believe in death. In the multiverse, once you're possible, you exist. And once you exist, you exist forever one way or another. Besides, death is the absence of life, and the ghosts I've met are very much alive. What we call ghosts are lifeforms just as you and I are. ~Paul F. Eno, Footsteps in the Attic)

Peculiar Occurrences at the Oddity Store

What appears to be just another white two-story home along a busy road, is a lot more than it looks. If you slow down and take a closer look, you would notice a public parking lot as well as an "open" sign in the window. This is not a residence but Wilmington's Oddity / Antique store. On the corner of Marsh and Sherwood Roads, this house is coated in a wonderful shade of mature trees that line the streets as well as the whole neighborhood. Upon closer examination, you will notice this is the obscure but well-known "Oddporium, the Gallery of the Peculiar and the Bizarre" store. This is a two-section store, with a gold dealer in one part and the oddity store in the other. Converted from the owner's former childhood home, this is where you need to go to pick up everything from human skulls to funeral items as well as Victorian elixirs, concoctions, and bottles of potions that were promoted to heal all ills.

The store is owned by decedents of the original builder of the home, and many generations have lived and died in this location. The structure was built in 1911, by Harry Harrison, who was the great-great-uncle of the store-owner, Ken Schuler. Ken and his bride, Elizabeth Busch now run the store in the rooms that were once occupied by the family members who had passed away many years before. For example, Harry Harrison's wives both died on the premises. First, he lost Mary to tuberculosis, whose remains are now buried in the back yard. Then there was the death of the second wife, named Winnie, who died in an upstairs room from lung cancer but received a normal funeral burial. Many other family members have died including the strange death of "Uncle Frank," who died while entering the home. Also a selection of great-great family members have taken their last breath on the premise. In total, seven members have died on the property over the years. So the house itself could hold many spirits on its own, but with the vast collection of macabre items, who knows how many items hold a form of attachment?

Several customers who have been to the upstairs gallery have had coughing fits while upstairs. Once the people leave the room, they return to their normal selves, and all signs of coughing come to an end. The owners have tried to find an explanation but to no avail. Could this have anything to do with the two women that died from lung disease and the spirits are causing guests to feel the pain they felt right before they died?

Shadow figures seem to roam the premises and have been witnessed by patrons and renters alike. These images are mainly in the front and rear gallery. In recent years many customers have said they have witnessed a shadow moving behind the coffin that lies on display in one of the showrooms. The same shadows have been seen in other rooms, and in some instances, it takes the shape of a human figure. When Ken was alerted to this phenomena, it brought back memories of when he was a child, and his uncle would take trips out of town. Ken's job as a young boy was to enter his uncle's home and turn on a couple of lights before darkness fell. In the morning, Ken would run back across the street and turn off the lights. The following night, he would turn on different lights. This gave the impression that someone was home during the night-time hours.

Ken's memory of turning on the lights one evening lead to him recalling a time when he was almost back to his home when he glanced back to the house, and in total horror, he witnessed a person standing in the upstairs bedroom window. This scared him to the core as he thought there was a stranger in the house while he turned on lights. He told his parents who later told him there was no one in the house. This shadow-man would appear solid in form to passers-by who observed this faceless apparition standing still within the window frame. Ken and Elizabeth have grown used to this shadow person moving around their store and now accept it as part of the character of the building. Most haunted locations would be happy with this amount of activity, but this is just the start of the dark tales of this store.

With the exception of items flying off the walls and artifacts moving of their own free will, there is one item that sits on a shelf in the store that has a legend of her own. It is a scary looking Victorian doll that had eyes that would close once she is laid on her back. The mystery with this doll occurs when a customer would lay her down, and the eyes close. Nothing special about that, right? Correct, but it is when the doll winks at the customer who is staring at her. This has been reported on many occasions, and this is enough to aid the customers on a rapid exit of the location.

Many times people report adult males having conversations in the back rooms of the building, but Ken and Beth know there is no one back there. It is well known that most guests to the store have a feeling of doom and are very afraid once entering a room on the upper floor. There is no evidence of any paranormal activity in the room, but that feeling of sadness engulfs almost everyone that approaches.

When paranormal groups take any photos, it always has orbs and streaks in their photos. Maybe the amount of dust that is kicked up when people enter the room or could it be more than just the need for a spring clean?

One night Beth was alone in the store while doing inventory, she started to feel uneasy, and from out of the blue, the windows started to slam shut. Doors throughout the house were flung open, and the cabinet doors sprung open with this all occurring at the same time. This was enough to scare the living daylights out of Beth, so she ran out onto the porch and waited for Ken to get back from his delivery. She would not go back into the house until she was fully sure that there was nothing malevolent in the home. Since that incident, Beth has installed a rather heavy bookshelf in front of one door, just in case it wants to start swinging widely for no apparent reason. This particular door was checked over, and nothing was wrong with it, and there seemed to be no reason for it to fly open so aggressively.

Some of the activity that goes on in the store can be related back to family members who watch out over Ken and Beth. A great example of the family looking out for them was the night that the owners were relaxing at home watching television and then they receive a call saying the alarm system was going off and it indicates there is an intruder on the premises. Ken jumps in the car and grabs a flashlight on his way out of the house. Once he pulled up into the driveway, he was met by the local police who were already looking in the windows of the building. After explaining he was the owner, Ken gingerly unlocked the lock and pushed open the front door of the store. Peering into the darkness, Ken saw nothing out of the ordinary. Stepping inside, he slowly and quietly moved through the darkness, only to be confronted with a shimmer of a candle from a distant room. Now turning on the lights to the building, Ken picked up the pace and held his flashlight in a defensive manner. Entering the room where the glow was seen, he noticed a candle was still burning on a very delicate and flammable piece of material. The rest of the building was checked, and there was no sign of a break-in or the fact that anyone had been in the property since it was locked up hours before. Returning to the room that held the lit candle, Ken realized that he had forgot to blow out the candle before he left for the night and the candle had almost burnt out. As Ken reached down to extinguish the flame, the heat from the glass container was so hot that it burnt his hand. He quickly pulled his hand away and bent down to blow out the candle instead of picking it up. He then noticed the heat from the candle was starting to crack the glass, and if he had not stifled the flame, the glass would have broken, the wick would have fallen onto the table and a fire would have broken out, with the distinct possibility of the old wooden structure going up in flames, destroying valuable historic items as well as this historic structure. It may appear as a family member did not want their home to burn to the ground, or they wanted their family members business to remain intact.

EVP's or "Electronic Voice Phenomena" has become a major way many paranormal investigators make contact or allegedly communicate with the dead. Most often, EVPs have been captured on audiotape. The mysterious voices are not heard at the time of recording; it is only when the tape is played back that the voices are heard. Sometimes amplification and noise filtering is required to hear the voices. EVP is a mysterious event in which human-sounding voices from an unknown source are heard on recording tape, in radio station noise and other electronic media. Some EVP are more easily heard and understood than others. And they vary in gender (men and women), age (adults and children), tone and emotion. They usually speak in single words, phrases, and short sentences. Sometimes they are just grunts, groans, growling and other vocal noises. EVP has been recorded speaking in various languages. Many of these recordings that have been collected from the oddity store on Marsh Road, and many people including EVP expert, Danny Reimer of the "Delaware Researchers of the Paranormal," believe they have caught the voice of a passed soul who wants to have their voice heard just one last time. It is well known to the people that personally know Beth, that Beth has a tendency not to stay focused for a long period of time. This appears to have been noticed by the dead as well as the living. On one set of

EVP's, you can hear a voice calling out to Beth to listen and focus. This happened a few times during a recording session with a local paranormal group on the premises. Later the voice says " Beth stay focused," this time the voice seemed agitated. When a sensitive in the group asked how this spirit knew Beth, an instant response came back in a very angry voice that said " F#@k You Beth." The voice was not heard again that night.

The final example that comes from the house leads back over 30 years ago when a close friend and Ken were in cub scouts together. Ken's friend said that he was going to die by killing himself. Ken did not think much of this statement as he was also a young 10-year old boy and boys that age are known to say some of the craziest things to get attention. As the boys got older and grew up together, they both attended the same high school and once more the same comment from many years before came up in a conversation that Ken's friend would die by suicide in a few years. At this age, it was clear that there was a form of mental illness that needed to be addressed. The worry of a kid killing himself in the neighborhood faded away for many years until one night after a party, Ken's childhood friend was found not breathing in the back garden of the store, which was still a home at that time. The premonitions and warnings had finally come true. This great friend had ended his life in sight of his good friends home. Once the body was removed, and an official police investigation was concluded, the police tape was removed, there was no sign of anything unusual happening in the yard. The only thing that stood there was a large tree. To this day when paranormal groups investigate the store, many times, the true physics and mediums will always be drawn to one spot in the back yard. It appears in one spot there is a happy feeling but you move to another area, and there is the feeling of sadness. It was noted that the site of the sadness and the exact spot of the joyful feeling are the exact spots that the ashes of the great- great grandmother was laid to rest and the other location is the site of the suicide. The locations will remain unpublished to help prevent vandals and wannabe ghost hunters wandering the private property.

On a personal note, I had made a phone call to Ken and Beth, and while talking to them, I made a comment " That is a very unusual thing to happen isn't it" and over the phone line came a very clear voice that drowned out Ken which said very clearly and in a deep voice " Yes, Very Unusual". Rather spooky I would say.

Due to the high amount of paranormal activity from this location, SyFy Channel's "Ghost Hunters" were called in to do an investigation of the Rockwood Mansion that housed a display of artifacts from the "Oddporium, the Gallery of the Peculiar and the Bizarre." The show aired on Halloween week of 2016, and the conclusion was that the building and its items did, in fact, have paranormal activity connected to them.

("Reality is merely an illusion, albeit a very persistent one."
— Albert Einstein)

Bank Deposits Remain

Steve has lived in the State of Delaware most of his life. Being an avid writer and fitness fanatic, he found himself in peak physical condition from many years of weightlifting and the martial arts. This young man had now graduated high school and found himself working local jobs around the area. On a particular day, he heard about a position for a security officer for a company in Wilmington Delaware. He knew with his physical abilities, getting this position would not be a problem for him. This turned out to be true, and Steve was offered a position at the age of 20 years old. Very proud of what he had accomplished, he jumped right into training and managed to learn the position at a rapid rate.

Training was completed, and Steve awaited his first work assignment. He got the call that he was joining a team that monitored a bank complex in Wilmington. This would be a 30-minute drive, and his shift would be 10 pm till 6 am, and the building was in one of the more undesirable neighborhoods in the area. The area was known for robberies and other violent activities. There was also the high possibility of an attempted bank raid loomed large. The fear of humans was not the only thing that showed up while working this assignment.

It was within a week of having to patrol the aging hallways of this old location that Steve started to get an uneasy feeling as he walked the passageways. The feeling would come and go, as if he was walking through an invisible curtain of sorts. The feeling of the air getting heavy and pressing on his body in a way a heavy blanket would do when you are sleeping. This feeling would pass once he moved a few more steps, and he would lose his instant fear. It was like a rollercoaster of emotions and sensations as he walked his beat. This fear of walking into another field of pressure started to wear on Steve, but he was reluctant to say anything to anyone else, as it could jeopardize his job and his standing in the company. He surely did not want to report this to his supervisor.

Time passes, and Steve has worked his way up in the company and was now more respected as a competent guard. This allowed him the chance to talk to his peers on a level that would not seem like a scared rookie. When sitting in the break room with a co-worker, he brought up the subject of ghosts and if anyone believes? He never let on that he had experienced many things in his time in the bank, but what he was doing was leading others to open up about any experiences over the years. Once the conversion was moving along at a steady pace, one officer said he had the feeling that there were ghosts in the building that they patrolled, even though he had never seen any. When asked why he thought there were ghosts, he replied that there is a heavy feeling throughout the buildings he worked and he also mentioned the feeling of being watched. With this revelation, other people started to share the guard's sentiments. It appeared that everyone that worked there had the feeling they were being watched too. It was then that Steve spoke up and said he too had the same feelings. Many of the men had the same experience in the same areas, but no one could explain why. Many of them put it down to the high stress of guarding a bank in a bad neighborhood. After this encounter with his team-mates, the conversation continued onto other stories, and the matter was put to rest. Everyone except Steve put it to rest. Weeks passed, and when Steve was walking the dark halls, he observed what was called "The Bridge." The Bridge was a glass-raised walkway that crossed from one building to another. This walkway was about 3 stories above the street and was framed in huge glass windows and decorative columns. As you approached this area of the building, you would start to get what is called a "Fun House" experience. This is when light and shadow causes you to feel off balance or out of sorts. Once you are entering the bridge, you will lose that feeling and be able to look side to side and see the street traffic passing below. This would offer a feeling of being in the open air and rather different from the stale hallways and doorways of the old buildings. Steve crossed this bridge on a nightly basis while doing his rounds and thought nothing of it until one night when he had felt the heavy pressure on his body. He approached the lighted bridge area when he was taken aback by what appeared to be a person in the shadows of the pillars approximately 15 to 20 feet in front of him. This caused an instant reaction to go on the defense and Steve took a few large steps backward and held his ground. Taking out his flashlight, he scanned the area and called out to the person he saw peeking out from behind the pillar. There was no answer, and no one stepped forward to admit to being in the building. Still scanning with his flashlight, Steve slowly and carefully stepped forward. One foot in front of the other, he encountered the area where this person was seen. He was shocked to see no one there and no way a human could have hidden behind that column. This caused him to high tail out of the area and back to his base office. Upon making it back to the office, Steve took a seat and hung his head and tried to make sense of what he had just seen. Even though Steve was required to finish his tour, he kept playing over in his mind every step that happened minutes before.

As the sun rose from behind the other buildings, the shift was over, and Steve had made it home safely when he recalled a conversation he had while walking the hallways with another guard a few weeks before. He stated he had witnessed what looked like a person on the same bridge; causing him to react in the same way as Steve, and no one was present when this guard called out. This made Steve realize he was not losing his mind and what was going on in the building was real to him and everyone else working the night shift.

Within a week, Steve was on duty with the same guard who told him of his shadow person encounter when they compared notes as they walked through the building. It was then made clear to Steve that there were many more haunting stories throughout the bank. Steve was told of an encounter of a cleaning person who took off her shoes when entering a carpeted room in the upper suites. She placed the shoes neatly by the opened door. And within moments of returning to the door, her shoes were gone. The woman thought it was a prank until the shoes were found further in the room she was working in. There was no way anyone could have been in the same room as she was working without her seeing them. It could be a tall tale or proof that there is more than just images wandering the halls with the cleaners and the guards.

So you would think that is the end of this story, but you are wrong. It was not days later that Steve was back on the night shift and he approached an area where he and others had experienced cold spots as well as the heavy feelings. Steve wondered if this thing would make itself visible to him on this night. Slowly walking forward, he felt the pressure build on his body, and then he started to get short of breath as the air was getting heavy once more. Continuing to slowly step forward, he then felt what was described as someone brushing past him; in a fast pace, enough to cause a nudge on Steve's shoulder. But the thing that made this interaction extremely nerve racking was the fact he heard a clear

whisper in his ear that said: " You're Going To Die."
Even though Steve is able to look after himself in most
situations, this was not one of them. He turned and ran
back to the safety of the office, where he bust in and sat
quietly in the corner trying to rationalize this now
aggressive spirit.

After months of patrolling the halls of the bank,
nothing compared to the whisper in the ear, even though
there were a few reports of shadow people on the bridge
as well as cold spots and heavy air. Things were not
causing Steve the nervousness and fear they had in the
past, and it appeared that the evil entity had given up on
Steve. One day, two officers were sitting in a room
taking a break. Steve was present and relaxing during
his shift when one of the others brought up religion and
how it affects the living and the dead. The conversation

was in full swing when the officer said a few things that were very inappropriate to anyone that was listening at the time. All the people in the room reacted in a negative manner over his statements. But it appeared that it was not just the living that was upset with this man's words. It was then that all the men in the room jumped from their seats to react to the sound of heavy boots stomping across the room, from behind Steve to the far end of the room in front of Steve's position. All the men were left dumbfounded and speechless. All were looking at each other and trying to understand what had happened. Then came the sounds of someone pounding on all four walls and the feeling of confusion within the men. As before, all the men quickly exited the room and congregated outside to have a smoke and try and decide what they would tell their supervisor.

Steve (not his real name), continues to work in the field of security and has had other experiences in different locations, but the shock of the 6 feet tall shadow man peeking at him and the hateful whisper caused him to forever remember the details of those nights.

("The more enlightened our houses are, the more their walls ooze ghosts. - Italo Calvino)

Conclusion

So what originally started out as a book based on one individual and his experiences; finally, became a collection of telephone and e-mail interviews regarding personal experiences with the unknown from many different people. What started out to be based in the State of Delaware, lead to stories from Ohio, Illinois, Pennsylvania and even Europe. What started as a way of thanking a person that I had known for years became a new quest to air the views of many people that had no outlet to tell their own story.

Life is too short to worry about petty things in life. Your life may end today or tomorrow. No one knows the exact moment your soul will leave this Earth. You must make the most of what lies ahead of you and greet it with open arms.

Thanks to some nervous reaction based on the idea of this book, it has led me to a group of new friends and people who are down to earth and wonderful. I have been told so many stories, that I had to limit to this collection. There is enough for a second edition, but we will have to see if there is enough interest in the subject to create more. It takes a strong person with a lot of trust to open up to a stranger on the other end of a phone line. It takes even more trust to allow that stranger to put their story into print, and for that, I thank everyone mentioned in the book.

Sometimes the attention and the acknowledgment of others can lead the mind to play tricks on the body. Some people try way too hard to find that one ghost photo or that one voice recording. This field was not built on shallow and weak evidence. Circling a dust cloud or a grain in the wood is not paranormal. The field is built on the unexplained; the images the skeptics look at and hold their mental reaction for a few seconds while studying the images. The silence of a skeptic who closes their eyes and takes in the voices they hear on a recorder. The moment a skeptic has to think hard about what they have to say, is the time that you may be discovering there is more to death than dying. Of my ten years as a promoter of haunted locations located all across America, I have a tiny collection of unexplained paranormal photos and voice recordings. Tens of thousands of images and recordings have been cast aside and forgotten, but it's that 0.5% that makes me a believer of sorts.

So is the paranormal real, or is it a figment of our imagination? I say the paranormal is real, but only in limited cases. People are so eager to experience the paranormal, any creaking window, the whistle of wind or a shadow of a passerby could be misconstrued as a ghost. The introduction of television; even though sparked an interest in the field, has also watered down what could have been an educational tool, which has now been replaced with a 30-minute scripted comedy show.

The stories that have been offered to me are given in good faith. I cannot say if the stories are real, a figment of a wild imagination or just a call for attention, but what I do know is that when I offered the questions for the book, I received what I expect to be the truth and publish the wording as offered to me. All the stories have been reviewed and verified to see if ghosts were involved in some way, I leave that up to you.

If you have a story that you wish to share, please contact the folks at The Oddporium, The Gallery of the Peculiar and the Bizarre. Leave them your e-mail and a brief description of your story. This will then be relayed to California where I can call and set up an interview for the next installment of this series. Also look out for the series to include other states.

Thank you all for taking the time to read these short stories. If it was not for the paranormal community, I would not be where I am now in life.

("Monsters are real, and ghosts are real too. They live inside us, and sometimes they win."STEPHEN KING, attributed, A Book of Horrors)